The information described herein is for educational purposes only. Neither the author nor the publisher take responsibility for any effects that may result from using these techniques: the readers do so at their own risk. Always seek the help of a medical professional for diagnosis or treatment of illness or injury.

ISBN: 1-4392-3146-X
LCCN: 2009902205
EAN13: 9781439231463

**www.secretgardenreiki.com**

# INTRODUCTION

You are about to take a journey into
the world of beautiful energy healing called

## "REIKI"

The information you will be given
comes from a direct line of masters
referred to as a "lineage".

My  lineage is:
Usui, Hayashi, Takata, Gray, Rosenthal.
I teach the Usui Shiki Ryoho method
of Reiki and am a member of The Reiki Alliance.

Welcome to the world of
## UNIVERSAL ENERGY HEALING.
Enjoy the journey!

# DEDICATION

To all the dear "angels" in my life.

To my husband Jim, four sons
and daughters-in-law.

To our grandchildren:
Abigaile, James, Ryan, Michael
Amanda, John, Isabella,
Alex and Cameron,

They have taught me
much more than I could
ever have taught them
and have filled my heart
with so much joy & love.

# ACKNOWLEDGEMENTS

To Chris Rosenthal, my Reiki Master, mentor & friend.

And to the lineage Masters who have passed down their Reiki instructions and knowledge... Thank you!

To my dear friends:  Hazel & Dawn for editing
and to Linda & Alanna for being there.

To Gary LaCoste for his professional advice
and guidance.

4

# WHAT IS REIKI?
Reiki is pronounced:

**Ray**

**Key**

Rei: Knowledge of spiritual consciousness

Ki: Vital life force or universal life force

Reiki is a Japanese word

# WHAT IS A LIFE FORCE?
A life force is the energy in all living things.

People

Animals

Trees/Plants
Fruit/Berries

Reiki healing energy
can be given to anyone
and anything we touch.

## WHAT DOES REIKI DO?

Reiki is a form of healing energy that comes
from the universe and then through us.

Reiki healing energy can be given
to anyone or anything we touch
through the palms of our hands.

Reiki is beautiful.
Reiki is love.
Reiki always goes for
the highest good.

# HOW DOES REIKI ENERGY KNOW WHERE TO GO?

Because

Reiki is beautiful,

Reiki is love,

Reiki always goes for the highest good.

## REIKI CAN HEAL ON MANY LEVELS

Body      Mind      Feelings      Spirit

Energy centers inside
our bodies are called:
"Chakras"

10

# WHAT IS ENERGY?

Energy is vitality, force, vigor, dynamics, pep,
spirit, output, resonance, potency,
motivity, strength, etc.

# WHERE IS ENERGY?

Energy is everywhere... in us and around us.
Each of the energy centers

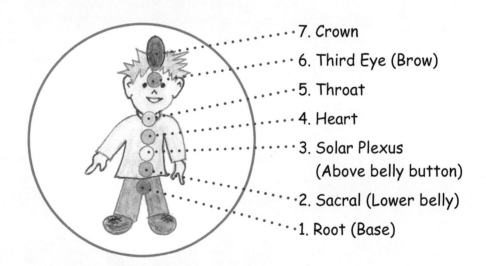

7. Crown

6. Third Eye (Brow)

5. Throat

4. Heart

3. Solar Plexus
(Above belly button)

2. Sacral (Lower belly)

1. Root (Base)

inside our bodies is called a **"Chakra"**
Chakra is pronounced: **Chuhk Ruh**
There are **Seven Major Chakras** inside our bodies.

The energy outside of
our body is called the
"Aura"

The energy outside of our body is called the
**"AURA"**

Aura is pronounced: **Oar   Ruh**

Energy is: "Inside us"

Energy is: "Around us"

Energy is: "Everywhere

Energy is everywhere.

# HOW DO WE GET REIKI?

Remember that energy is "everywhere" and
available to all of us.

Inside & outside our bodies.
Inside & outside our world.
This is called:

## "UNIVERSAL ENERGY"

**Try this:**
Rub your hands together and then separate them.
Pretend you are holding an invisible ball.

As you move them away from each other
and back together... feel the

## "ENERGY"

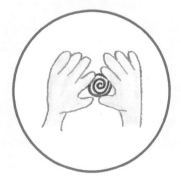

Sound, images with color,
come from frequencies,
energy waves and vibrations
that are "everywhere".

# DID YOU EVER WONDER?

How does a cell phone connect us to the
number that we have dialed?
How does a computer access information from
very long distances?
How does a radio or television get sound or
images with colors in a split second?

# THE ANSWER

From the frequencies,
energy waves,
and vibrations that are
"everywhere".
You know that we have these waves of energy
inside and outside our bodies
(chakras & auras)
that affect how we feel and give us life.

We also have frequencies and energy waves and
vibrations all around us and in space.

We can "feel" the
frequencies, energy waves,
and vibrations.

# WHAT ARE FREQUENCIES, ENERGY WAVES AND VIBRATIONS?

The energy waves are what
enable us to "tap" into each other,
to communicate or talk to each other,
and to receive information.

This is done by electrical towers,
cell towers, satellite dishes, space satellites, etc.

Examples of waves or vibrations can
be seen in how music makes us feel.

The resonance or vibration of the
notes and melody travel through the
air and we react to the frequency
by dancing, singing, tapping, and
moving to the beat.

We can "feel" the vibration or
**"ENERGY"**

A Reiki Master knows how
to activate the energy so it will
flow to us and through us
from the universe.

# HOW DO WE PLUG INTO REIKI ENERGY?

We can "tap" into this universal energy to
use for Reiki healing after we have been
"plugged in", or connected, by a Reiki Master
using special symbols that have been passed
on from master to master and then to you.
The masters knows how to activate or
plug us into the energy so that it will
flow to us and through us
from the universe.
This is done in a very special ritual,
or ceremony, through attunements, also
known as initiations, and are sacred mysteries,
or "keys" that make the Reiki healing energy
available to you always.

You will always have the
healing energy available
to you, anywhere
and anytime.

# WHO CAN DO REIKI?

**Anyone can do Reiki.**

Once attuned by a Reiki Master,
the healing energy will flow through
you to whomever or whatever you touch.

# IS REIKI EASY TO LEARN?

**Yes! Even for a child.**

You do not have to know anything!
You do not have to believe in anything!
You do not have to think!
You do not have to use your own energy!
You will always have the healing energy
available to you, anywhere and anytime.

The Reiki energy
will always be available to you
and will never go away.

# WILL THE "REIKI ENERGY" EVER GO AWAY?

No... the Reiki energy will never go away.

Once you have been attuned, you
will always have the Reiki healing energy
available to you.

## BE HAPPY AND HEALTHY

Let go of anger
Let go of worry
Be thankful for everyone and everything
in your life.
Always do the best you can in
everything you do
Be kind and thoughtful to everyone.

Reiki will help you to stay
balanced and help you make
better decisions and choices
in your life.

# STAY HAPPY AND HEALTHY

Smile and laugh a lot.

Eat what is good for you
like fruits and
vegetables

Try to avoid junk foods.
Drink plenty of water.
Drink juices and milk.
Get plenty of rest & sleep.

Get plenty of exercise
and lots of fresh air.

Have good hygiene.

Reiki attunements will balance you
and help you to stay away from
habits that would not be good for you.
You will be able to make better
decisions and choices.

Doing Reiki on yourself every
day will help you to stay
balanced and centered.

# HOW WILL DOING REIKI ON MYSELF HELP?

Doing Reiki on yourself every day
will help you to stay balanced
and centered.
It will help to keep the vital energy
force in your body moving so you
can be healthy and happy.

## REIKI  HEAD POSITIONS

Eyes

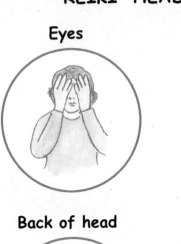

Temples

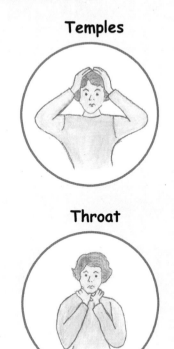

Back of head

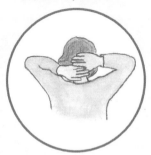

Throat

Reiki will help to keep the
vital energy force in your
body moving so you can be
healthy and happy.

# REIKI BODY POSITIONS

## Front of body

### Heart

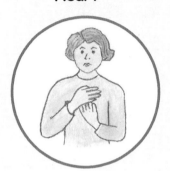

### Front  positions

## Back of body

### Shoulders

### Back positions

Reiki was rediscovered by a man
from Japan named
Mikao Usui
in the early 1900's.

# WHERE DID REIKI COME FROM?

Reiki was rediscovered by a man
named Mikao Usui in the country of
Japan in the early 1900's.
He was a wonderful student and
knew about history, medicine, psychology,
scriptures, etc, and he meditated regularly.
He had decided to go to Mt. Kurama,
near Kyoto, Japan, for a 21 day intensive
meditation to seek enlightenment.
He kept track of the days with 21 stones and
on the last day, the wonderful symbols and
mysteries of Reiki came to him.
He soon realized how special this was
and began sharing the healing energy
with many people all over Japan.
He also taught and shared
what he knew to others so
they could do the same.

**Mikao Usui**

Dr. Chujiro Hayashi
carried on the healing work
and teachings of Mikao Usui.

# WHERE DID REIKI COME FROM?

(continued)

One of Mikao Usui's students was named
Dr. Chujiro Hayashi.

He was a retired surgeon commander
and medical doctor in the
Japanese Navy.
Dr. Hayashi carried on the
healing work of Usui and many came
to receive treatments. He also went
on to teach what he had learned.
One of his patients and students was
a woman named Hawayo Takata.
Dr. Hayashi came to the USA to help her
set up a Reiki clinic in Hawaii in 1937.
This is how Reiki found it's way out of Japan,
and it is now being practiced and taught
all over the world.

**Dr. Chujiro Hayashi**

Reiki is now found all
around the world thanks to
Hawayo Takata.

# WHERE DID REIKI COME FROM?
(continued)

Hawayo Takata was born in Hawaii in 1900.
She became a widow at a very early age
and had the responsibility of raising her
two girls. She had severe physical problems
that could not be easily taken care of.
On a visit to Japan, Mrs. Takata
found Dr. Hayashi's clinic and,
after receiving Reiki treatments there,
she became well again.
Dr. Hayashi consented to teach
her the art of Reiki although passing
on knowledge to someone who was not
from Japan was not common
practice at that time. Takata, as she
liked to be called, went on to treat
many people all over the USA.
She also taught this beautiful healing
energy, called Reiki, to many.

Reiki is now found all around the world,
thanks to Hawayo Takata.

**Hawayo Takata**

When there is an injury,
Reiki is a wonderful thing
to do right away.

# IMPORTANT TO REMEMBER

When there is an injury, Reiki
is a wonderful thing to do
right away.
Put your hand on the injury, if you can,
for a few minutes.

It will help with pain and to heal quicker.

Reiki will never go away.

You don't have to know what the
problem is to do Reiki.

The more you do Reiki,
the stronger the energy will
become and the better
it will work.

Always trust yourself.
Reiki is never wrong and can
only do good.

# IMPORTANT TO REMEMBER
### (continued)

If you do not "feel" anything in
your hands, that is o.k.

The Reiki is still working.

Always trust yourself.

Reiki is never wrong and can only do good.

You are not using your own energy so you
will not get tired.

Remember to do Reiki on yourself often.

Try to do it every day if possible.

It is not necessary to "show off' your beautiful
gift of Reiki.

It's more important that
you help yourself and others.

Some people may not understand Reiki and
that's o.k.  We are all different and do not
think the same way and that is what
makes our world such a beautiful
and interesting place.

Made in the USA
Columbia, SC
23 January 2018